WHERE DID IT COME FROM?

INVENTING THE TOILET

by Emma Carlson Berne

Consultant: Beth Gambro
Reading Specialist, Yorkville, Illinois

BEARPORT PUBLISHING

Bearcub Books, an imprint of Bearport Publishing by FlutterBee

Teaching Tips

Before Reading

- Look at the cover of the book. Discuss the picture and the title.
- Ask readers to brainstorm a list of what they already know about toilets. What can they expect to see in the book?
- Go on a picture walk, looking through the pictures to discuss vocabulary and make predictions about the text.

During Reading

- Read for purpose. Encourage readers to think about what led to the need for toilets as they are reading.
- Ask readers to look for the details of the book. What were the first toilets like?
- If readers encounter an unknown word, ask them to look at the sounds in the word. Then, ask them to look at the rest of the page. Are there any clues to help them understand?

After Reading

- Encourage readers to pick a buddy and reread the book together.
- Ask readers to name two things that happened as the toilet was being invented. Find the pages that tell about these things.
- Ask readers to write or draw something they learned about toilets.

Credits
Cover and title page, © Pixel-Shot/Shutterstock; 3, © Best_photo_studio/Shutterstock; 5, © Cylonphoto/iStock; 6-7, © De Agostini/Getty Images; 9, © Bettmann Archive/Getty Images; 11, © IanDagnall Computing/Alamy Stock Photo; 13, © SSPL/Science Museum/Getty Images; 15, © World History Archive/Alamy Stock Photo; 17, © MOLA/Getty Images; 19, © The Print Collector/Alamy Stock Photo; 20–21, © Aleksia/Alamy Stock Photo; 22T, © Lasse Johansson/Shutterstock; 22M, © v74/Shutterstock; 22B, © Andrey Popov/Adobe Stock; 23TL, © SViktoria/Shutterstock; 23TR, © NanoStockk/iStock; 23BL, © Grigvovan/Shutterstock; 23BR, © Gala Oleksenko/Shutterstock

See BearportPublishing.com for our statement on Generative AI Usage.

Library of Congress Cataloging-in-Publication Data is available at www.loc.gov or upon request from the publisher.

ISBN: 979-8-89577-590-5 (hardcover)
ISBN: 979-8-89577-770-1 (paperback)
ISBN: 979-8-89577-678-0 (ebook)

For more information, write to Bearport Publishing, 3500 American Blvd W, Suite 150, Bloomington, MN 55431.
Printed in the United States of America.

Contents

Flush!

I have to go to the bathroom.

Flush!

We all use toilets every day.

But where did toilets come from?

Early people dug pits in the ground for toilets.

Some made seats out of stone.

But these toilets were very dirty.

The **inventor** John Harington made the first **flush toilet**.

He wanted to send poop and pee away from his house.

He created his toilet in 1592.

John Harington

Harington named his toilet Ajax.

He wrote a book about it.

The queen even came to see how it worked!

Harington's toilet had a pan.

Waste went into the pan.

Pulling a **lever** opened a hole in the pan.

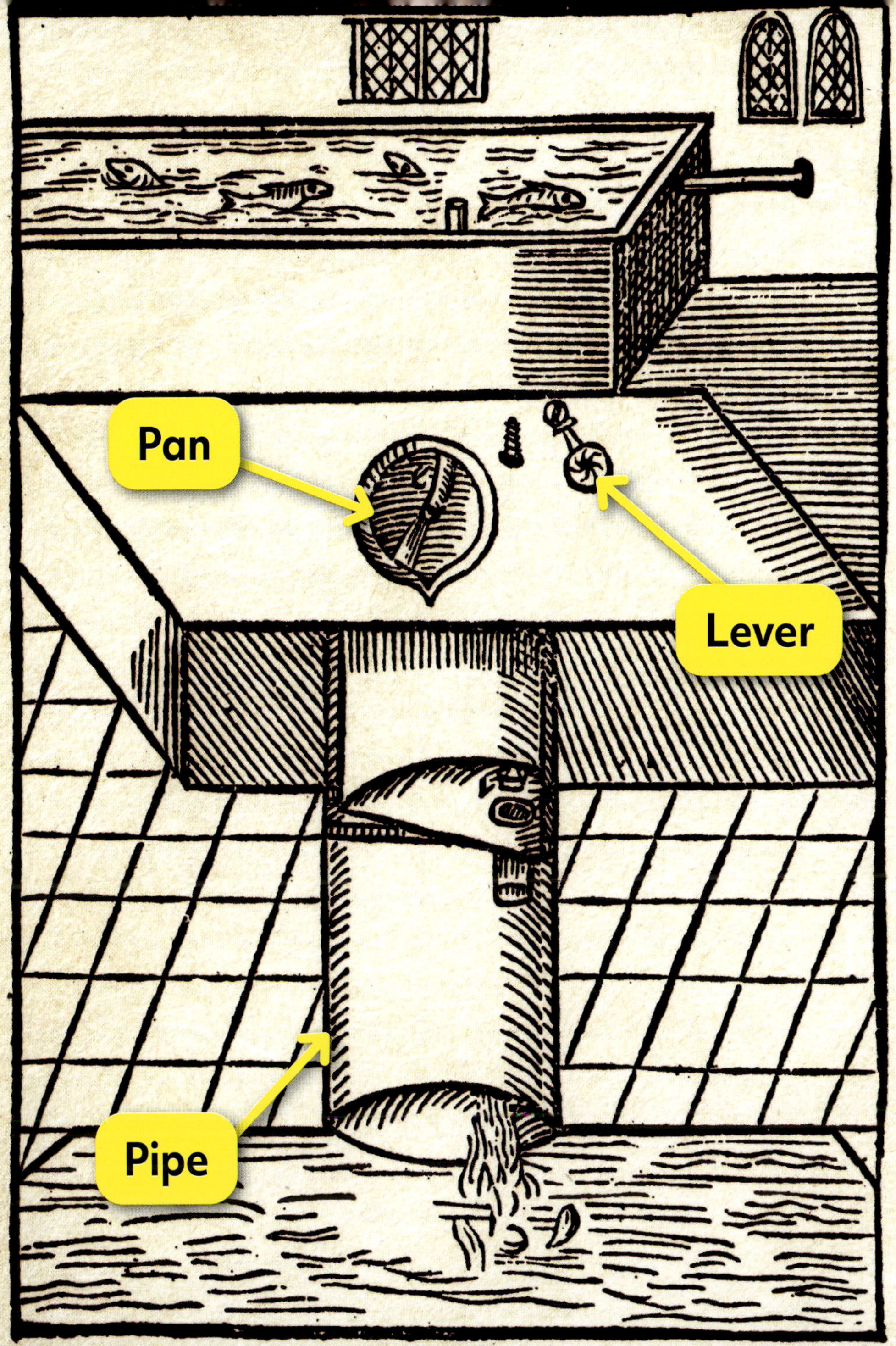
Pan
Lever
Pipe

The lever also sent water into the pan.

The water carried away the waste through a pipe.

The pipe emptied into a waste pit.

This was a hole in the ground.

Carrying waste away made John's toilet cleaner.

An old waste pit

Toilets kept changing over time.

They got less smelly.

And they cost less to buy.

By the 1940s, many people had toilets in their homes.

Toilets give us a clean place to pee and poop.

This helps keep us healthy.

Toilets are amazing!

Fun Toilet Facts

Some people still use outdoor toilets. These are called outhouses.

There are toilets in space! One sucks up waste and stores it in bags.

Most people use the toilet more than 2,000 times per year.

Glossary

flush toilet a toilet that uses water to move waste away

inventor someone who creates a thing for the first time

levers rods that move at a fixed point

waste trash or material not needed by the human body

Index

Read More

Bethea, Nicole Brooks. *Toilets (How Does It Work?).* Minneapolis: Jump! Pogo, 2021.

Murray, Julie. *Toilet (Best Inventions).* North Mankato, MN: Abdo Zoom, 2023.

Learn More Online

1. Go to **FactSurfer.com** or scan the QR code below.
2. Enter "**Inventing the Toilet**" into the search box.
3. Click on the cover of this book to see a list of websites.

About the Author

Emma Carlson Berne is the author of many books. She lives in Cincinnati, Ohio, with her husband, three children, one grumpy cat, and one friendly cat.